PRIORITY PLANNER & WELLNESS LOG

strategically simplify
to be your best this season

CONTENTS

HOW TO USE THIS 12-WEEK
PRIORITY PLANNER
& WELLNESS LOG

In this Planner, you'll have the opportunity to think through your personal goals and your overarching life-anchors. Solidifying these will help you to center your plans around your personal priorities and needs. The Priority Planner & Wellness Log contains the following entry-pages:

BIG PICTURE PRIORITIES
Make notes for the year, quarter, and month (you can break the 12 months down individually or into quarters as noted on page 13).

WEEK-AT-A-GLANCE
Log a brief recap of the previous week and strategically plan for the week ahead. Bring to mind your priority projects, relationships, and wellness goals in all the major areas of wellness as you think through your upcoming week's overarching focus, plans, events, & potential potholes.

To ask questions about Strong Snacks, Real Water, and sleep goals, head over to the RESOLVE group on Facebook!

JOURNAL/SKETCH PAGES
For reflection, these can be found before each week begins, & before each weekend.

DAILY PRIORITY PLANNING & WELLNESS LOGGING
Each day has sections for noting your intentions and actions simply and strategically, Monday through Sunday for 12 weeks. Setting SMART goals at the beginning of the week, along with daily planning, allows for purposeful urgency, balanced with intentional rest and recreation.

Set SMART goals:
Specific
Measurable
Attainable
Relevant
Time-bound

Example of a not-so-SMART goal:
Exercise more and eat fewer sweets.

Example of a SMART goal:
This week, exercise 5 of 7 days (30 min. each) & eat a maximum of two 200-calorie desserts: one on Tuesday and one on Saturday night.

*Need ideas for SMART goals? Request to join our private **RESOLVE** group on Facebook! We post our Monday goal weekly and follow-up for accountability throughout the week. Join us!*

MISSION MAP: **5Ps**

PRIORITIES

In order to best plan around your personal priorities, put some thought into what they are, and how they relate to each of the six areas of wellness noted below.

physical
relational
spiritual

personal
financial
professional

To decide what to prioritize over the next 12 weeks, consider the following final four "P"s:

PASSIONS

What gets you excited? What are you made to do? Who were you made to be?

PROJECTS

What's on your radar for this upcoming season? Go to the Big Picture Priorities calendar on page 13 to jot down your thoughts.

PROGRESS

Where do you need to see progress being made as it relates to your overall wellness? Note the following below:

WEIGHT	WAIST	CHOL	HDL	LDL	HGB/FER.	TRI	GLU/A1C	VIT D	THYROID

Date:

PEOPLE

Who are "your people"? This Planner prompts you to enjoy life with them strategically. Your people are those who are an integral part of your life: those who are bold enough to hold you accountable, and close enough to see the barriers and bumps in the road, encouraging you as they journey through life alongside you.

MAKE-A-PLAN MONDAY

Each Monday, note your SMART goal for the week. You will have the chance to report on progress later in the week. Utilize our private RESOLVE group on Facebook for accountability and camaraderie. It's helpful to partner with those with similar goals and challenges, and keeps your wellness walk fun and dynamic.

STRATEGICALLY SAVOR SLOWLY

Make a note of your strategically planned splurges considering what you see coming in the week ahead. Be honest with yourself on your daily splurge report (Monday through Sunday). Knowing what you're splurging on is key! Splurges are things like fried food, chips, heavy sauces, chocolate, candy and other desserts, and caloric beverages such as coffees, teas, sodas, energy drinks, sports drinks, wine, beer, and cocktails.

Triple **S** Strategy

MEMORIZE

Maximize the vitality of your mind, and make your day-to-day easier! Each week you can decide on something simple to memorize, if desired.

- Matthew 5:3-12 – The Beatitudes
- Your primary credit card number
- Your spouse's Social Security #
- Poetry
- Your friends' phone numbers
- Meaningful quotes
- Bible verse of the week
- Historical speeches
- Your bank account number
- Science and math facts
- Measurement conversions
- Sports stats

- Your license plate number
- The Lord's Prayer
- Historical facts (ex: presidents)
- Friends and family members' birthdays
- Your blood type
- Geographical landmarks
- States and and their capitals
- Planets and related facts
- The Prayer of St. Francis
- Foreign language vocabulary
- Definitions of challenging words
- Choreography (think Zumba)

TAKE 10 TUESDAY

Try a few of these every Tuesday for **10 minutes**:
Each day contains 96 back-to-back 10-minute increments. Make the most of them!

PHYSICAL

- Work on your posture
- Walk briskly or jog for 10 minutes
- Clean out your pantry
- Dance like no one is watching
- Do 10 minutes of stretching
- Disinfect light switches & doorknobs
- Use a foam roller
- Wash your face & moisturize your skin
- Prepare Strong Snacks for the week
- Prep herbs or limes for a fresh zing
- Use a hand or foot therapy ball
- Schedule an annual check-up
- Apply sunscreen
- Use a neti pot or saline mist
- Go to bed 10 minutes earlier
- Get up 10 minutes earlier
- Chop up fresh veggies & fruit for later
- Review your entries in this logbook
- Stash water bottles around your home, as well as in your office and car

RELATIONAL

- Call someone for a 10-minute chat
- Work on a difficult relationship
- Hand-write a note or card and mail it
- Snuggle your kids or grandkids
- Slow dance with your significant other
- Text 3 people what you love about them
- Forgive yourself and someone else
- Eat a romantic dinner by candlelight
- Strike up a conversation with a little child
- Schedule a weekly date night, or similar
- Wear something special or fancy
- Join a team, a support group, or hobbyists

FINANCIAL

- Set up a monthly budget
- Consign/sell a box of clothes or items
- Note your debt & make a plan to reduce it
- Plan how you'll prioritize giving & saving
- Write out a grocery list and/or a meal plan
- Check bills for unnecessary subscriptions

TAKE 10 TUESDAY

Check these off once you do them for
10 minutes on Tuesdays (or anytime)!

SPIRITUAL

- [ ] Morning devotional/meditation
- [ ] Journal your prayers
- [ ] Join a group to discuss meaningful matters
- [ ] Soak up sunshine and nature (try a walk through the park)
- [ ] Memorize a scripture verse each week
- [ ] Read your previous years' journals

PROFESSIONAL

- [ ] Put down your phone
- [ ] Set monthly goals
- [ ] Clear off your desk
- [ ] Breathe deeply
- [ ] Reach out to a mentor
- [ ] Make a list of things to delegate
- [ ] Set out your clothes & workout clothes
- [ ] Register to attend a training
- [ ] Schedule a vacation
- [ ] Write out a 5-year plan
- [ ] Communicate boundaries for work hours

PERSONAL

- [ ] Set a timer and watch funny videos
- [ ] Plant an herb garden
- [ ] Watch a sunrise or sunset
- [ ] Play your favorite song from high school
- [ ] Brew a cup of hot peppermint tea
- [ ] Give yourself a quick facial massage
- [ ] Take a bubble bath
- [ ] Do something creative
- [ ] Decide on your life value statement
- [ ] Walk or run in the grass barefoot
- [ ] Rock on your porch (or someone else's)
- [ ] Set up a reading plan & get the books
- [ ] Schedule a massage
- [ ] Light all the candles in your home
- [ ] Shut off your devices 10 minutes earlier
- [ ] Sing your favorite childhood song
- [ ] Review memorized scriptures/poems
- [ ] Take a power nap
- [ ] Pet a furry animal
- [ ] Take up a hobby or join a club
- [ ] Plan out your vacations for this year

WEDNESDAY: MID-WEEK METRIC CHECK

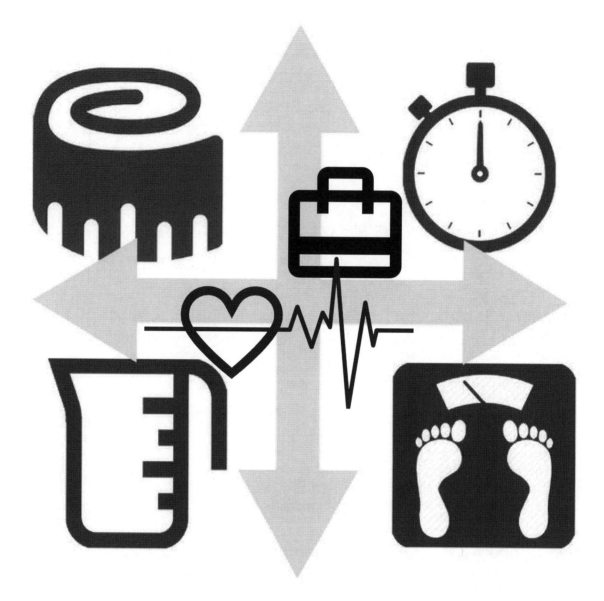

Each Wednesday, make notes of updates on measurable values (ex: waist measurement, lab values, etc.). Post your updates on the Mid-Week Metric Check thread on our RESOLVE Facebook group page.

EXAMPLES:

+ 10,000 steps
- 2 antacids
better blood sugar
+ 1 hour of sleep
- 20 sec./mile speed

+ 10 pounds on squats
- 2 ibuprofen
maintaining weight
- 1.5 pounds
+ 2 veggies

+ 1 water bottle
- 1 glass of wine
better blood pressure
- daily headache
- 1 laxative

THOUGHTFUL THURSDAY

Who should you check on this Thursdsay?

Enlist accountability and partnership whenever possible. We are truly #bettertogether. Life is just more rich that way: wellness is getting to enjoy life to its fullest with loved ones along for the ride.

Accountability is the secret sauce that turns knowledge into action. Knowledge really is not powerful without accountability to see it through. Invite others into your wellness walk:

- walk or jog with friends
- take classes and courses
- cook and eat together
- follow-up about follow-through
- travel & make memories
- encourage one another

FOLLOW-UP FRIDAY

Fridays are great for fun, and follow-up too! On Fridays, look back over the week's entries for personal AHA-moments. It will be a reporting day for the workweek.

Take time to evaluate: did you achieve your Make-a-Plan Monday goal over the weekdays? Jot down why or why not on Follow-Up Friday.

Self-assessment makes a significant difference in moving toward your goals. You can't fix what you don't recognize is broken: you can't maximize what you don't even realize!

Every Friday, jump on our RESOLVE group page on Facebook and share how your week went in terms of your priorities and goals (or phone a friend).

Fridays are perfect for preparing for a strategic and successful weekend. When it comes to healthy choices, people tend to negate their overall progress on the weekends (and often without noticing that's the problem).

Taking a few giant weekend-day leaps backward after the several small weekday steps taken to move forward brings only diminishing returns. Be sure to make notes on the Week-at-a-Glance page about what you see coming up so you aren't blindsided, and note your food and beverages.

RECIPE-SWAP SATURDAY

The weekend is an ideal time to swap recipes so you can prepare for the week ahead.

Jump on the RESOLVE group page on Facebook and look at the Saturday morning recipe-swap thread to build your recipes and menu plan for the week. After sharing some of your own favorite recipes, make a menu plan and grocery list for the upcoming week.

SLIP-IT-ON-SUNDAY

On Sundays, if you are aiming to manage your weight, rather than weighing or measuring more than once a week, just "slip on" some realistic, short-term "goal-pants" (that are free of spandex). This will give you an honest assessment without tempting you to obsess about the numbers, if that might be your tendency.

Share your Vents and Victories of the week with others in the Sunday comment thread on RESOLVE. Accountability and camaraderie might not be as critical on something like a 20-day diet, but our goal here is lifetime wellness: physical, personal, relational, spiritual, financial, and professional. Community makes it fun!

Sundays are perfect for reviewing the previous week. Keep in mind that on Wednesdays of each week you'll be evaluating the measurable aspects of wellness and noting any updates (Mid-Week Metric Check). On Follow-Up Fridays you'll review the previous weekdays. The Week-at-Glance planner page gives you the opportunity to note the previous week's wins, as well as what didn't work out as planned while you get prepared for the upcoming week.

Make the most of your Sundays by doing some food prep for the upcoming days. This can be good family fun, and it makes the week go by much more smoothly. Refer to the meal prep suggestions, recipes, and grocery lists in my *Best Body Cookbook & Menu Plan* to keep it simple.

BIG-PICTURE PRIORITIES

JANUARY	FEBRUARY	MARCH

1st quarter

APRIL	MAY	JUNE

2nd quarter

JULY	AUGUST	SEPTEMBER

3rd quarter

OCTOBER	NOVEMBER	DECEMBER

4th quarter

WEEK AT A GLANCE

OVERARCHING WEEKLY FOCUS

....

WINS FROM LAST WEEK

WHAT DIDN'T WORK?

THINGS TO GET DONE THIS WEEK:

THINGS TO GET:

THINGS TO GET RID OF:

THIS WEEK'S WORKOUTS

M ....

T ....

W ....

T ....

F ....

S ....

S ....

DATE NIGHT/QUALITY TIME

....

....

COMMIT TO MEMORY

I SEE THIS COMING:

....

....

STRATEGIC SPLURGES AHEAD

Triple
S
Strategy

"Patience, persistence, and perspiration make an unbeatable combination for success." -Napoleon Hill

MAKE-A-PLAN MONDAY

hello gorgeous

TODAY'S TOP 3 TASKS

LAST NIGHT'S
HOURS OF
SLEEP

○ ○ ○

○ ○ ○

○ ○ ○

○ ○ ○

REAL WATER

■ ■ ■ ■

✓ ✓ ✓ ✓

PRAY FOR:

PAY FOR:

GRATEFUL FOR:

MEALS

BREAKFAST

LUNCH

STRONG SNACK

DINNER

SMART GOAL FOR THE WEEK

MAKE IT COUNT MOVEMENT

WEEKLY FOCUS REMINDER

SPLURGE REPORT

TAKE 10 TUESDAY

Get it done today!

TODAY'S TOP 3 TASKS

....
....
....

PRAY FOR:

PAY FOR:

GRATEFUL FOR:

COMMIT TO MEMORY

TAKE 10 TODAY (PAGES 8-9)

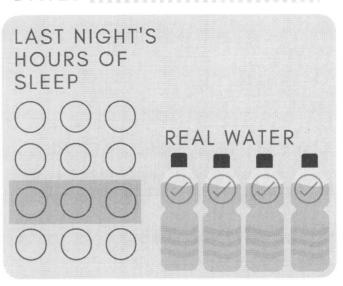

LAST NIGHT'S HOURS OF SLEEP

REAL WATER

MEALS

BREAKFAST

LUNCH

STRONG SNACK

DINNER

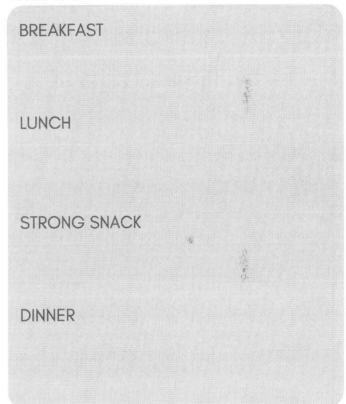

MAKE IT COUNT MOVEMENT

SPLURGE REPORT

WEDNESDAY
MID-WEEK METRIC CHECK
consistency is critical

TODAY'S TOP 3 TASKS

....
....
....

PRAY FOR:

PAY FOR:

GRATEFUL FOR:

COMMIT TO MEMORY

METRIC UPDATE

consistency is critical

DATE: ....

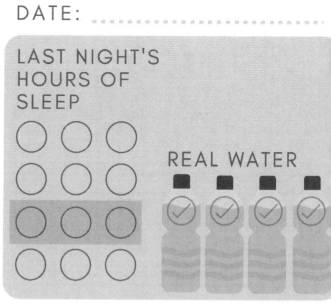

LAST NIGHT'S HOURS OF SLEEP

REAL WATER

MEALS

BREAKFAST

LUNCH

STRONG SNACK

DINNER

MAKE IT COUNT MOVEMENT

SPLURGE REPORT

THOUGHTFUL THURSDAY

friends are a treasure

TODAY'S TOP 3 TASKS

....

....

....

LAST NIGHT'S HOURS OF SLEEP

REAL WATER

PRAY FOR:

PAY FOR:

GRATEFUL FOR:

MEALS

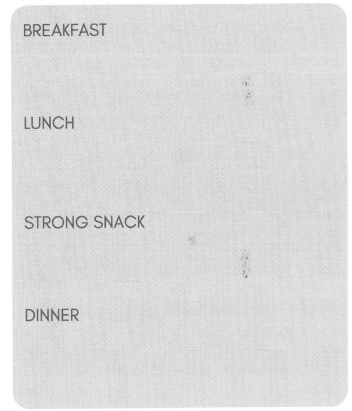

BREAKFAST

LUNCH

STRONG SNACK

DINNER

REACH OUT TO CHECK ON:

MAKE IT COUNT MOVEMENT

WEEKLY FOCUS REMINDER

SPLURGE REPORT

FOLLOW-UP FRIDAY

Yes you can!

TODAY'S TOP 3 TASKS

....

....

....

PRAY FOR:

PAY FOR:

GRATEFUL FOR:

COMMIT TO MEMORY

THIS WEEK'S GOAL UPDATE

DATE: ....

LAST NIGHT'S HOURS OF SLEEP

○ ○ ○
○ ○ ○
○ ○ ○
○ ○ ○

REAL WATER

MEALS

BREAKFAST

LUNCH

STRONG SNACK

DINNER

MAKE IT COUNT MOVEMENT

SPLURGE REPORT

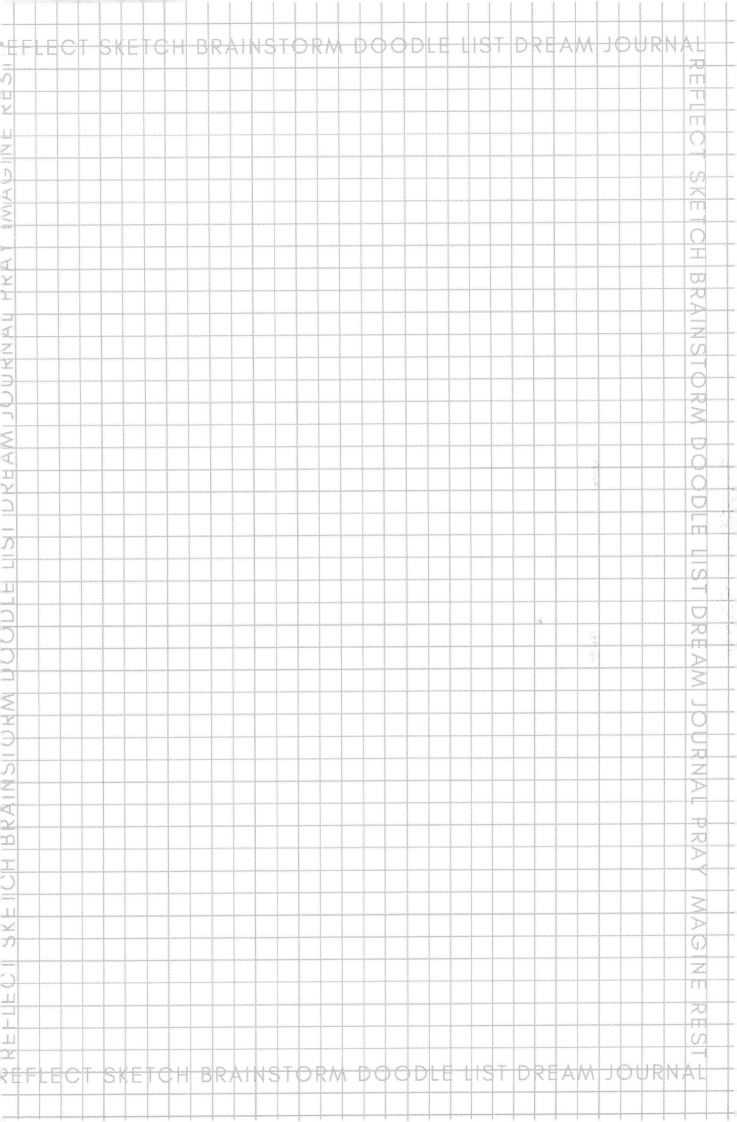

RECIPE-SWAP SATURDAY

share in R➡ESOLVE group

TODAY'S TOP 3 TASKS

....

....

....

LAST NIGHT'S HOURS OF SLEEP

REAL WATER

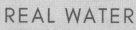
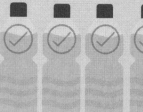

PRAY FOR:

PAY FOR:

GRATEFUL FOR:

MEALS

BREAKFAST

LUNCH

STRONG SNACK

DINNER

COMMIT TO MEMORY

MAKE IT COUNT MOVEMENT

WEEKLY FOCUS REMINDER

SPLURGE REPORT

SLIP-IT-ON SUNDAY

share in **RESOLVE** *group*

TODAY'S TOP 3 TASKS

. . . .

. . . .

. . . .

PRAY FOR:

PAY FOR:

GRATEFUL FOR:

COMMIT TO MEMORY

WEEKLY FOCUS REMINDER

DATE: . . . .

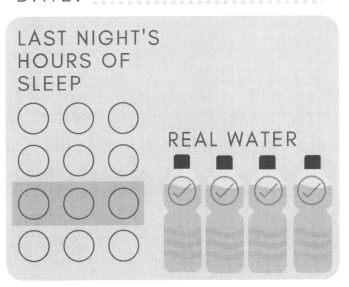

LAST NIGHT'S HOURS OF SLEEP

REAL WATER

MEALS

BREAKFAST

LUNCH

STRONG SNACK

DINNER

MAKE IT COUNT MOVEMENT

SPLURGE REPORT

WEEK AT A GLANCE

OVERARCHING WEEKLY FOCUS

WINS FROM LAST WEEK

WHAT DIDN'T WORK?

THINGS TO GET DONE THIS WEEK:

THINGS TO GET:

THINGS TO GET RID OF:

WEEK OF: ....

THIS WEEK'S WORKOUTS

M ....
T ....
W ....
T ....
F ....
S ....
S ....

DATE NIGHT/QUALITY TIME

....

....

COMMIT TO MEMORY

I SEE THIS COMING:

....

....

STRATEGIC
SPLURGES AHEAD

Triple
S
Strategy

"Some people WANT it to happen, some WISH it would
happen, others MAKE it happen." -Michael Jordan

MAKE-A-PLAN MONDAY

Rise and shine!

TODAY'S TOP 3 TASKS

....
....
....

PRAY FOR:

PAY FOR:

GRATEFUL FOR:

SMART GOAL FOR THE WEEK

WEEKLY FOCUS REMINDER

....

DATE: ....

LAST NIGHT'S HOURS OF SLEEP

REAL WATER

MEALS

BREAKFAST

LUNCH

STRONG SNACK

DINNER

MAKE IT COUNT MOVEMENT

SPLURGE REPORT

TAKE 10 TUESDAY

Mornin' sunshine!

TODAY'S TOP 3 TASKS

....

....

....

PRAY FOR:

PAY FOR:

GRATEFUL FOR:

COMMIT TO MEMORY

TAKE 10 TODAY (PAGES 8-9)

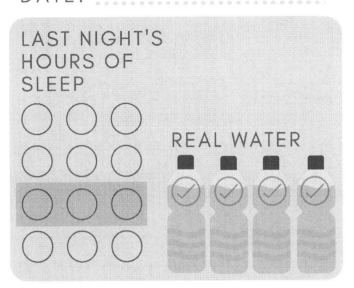

LAST NIGHT'S HOURS OF SLEEP

REAL WATER

MEALS

BREAKFAST

LUNCH

STRONG SNACK

DINNER

MAKE IT COUNT MOVEMENT

SPLURGE REPORT

WEDNESDAY
MID-WEEK METRIC CHECK

assess but don't obsess

TODAY'S TOP 3 TASKS

....
....
....

PRAY FOR:

PAY FOR:

GRATEFUL FOR:

COMMIT TO MEMORY

METRIC UPDATE

DATE: ....

LAST NIGHT'S HOURS OF SLEEP

○ ○ ○
○ ○ ○
○ ○ ○
○ ○ ○

REAL WATER

■ ■ ■ ■
✓ ✓ ✓ ✓

MEALS

BREAKFAST

LUNCH

STRONG SNACK

DINNER

MAKE IT COUNT MOVEMENT

SPLURGE REPORT

THOUGHTFUL THURSDAY

investing in relationship is priceless

TODAY'S TOP 3 TASKS

....

....

....

PRAY FOR:

PAY FOR:

GRATEFUL FOR:

REACH OUT TO CHECK ON:

WEEKLY FOCUS REMINDER

DATE: ....

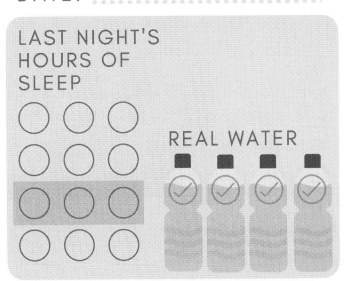

LAST NIGHT'S HOURS OF SLEEP

REAL WATER

MEALS

BREAKFAST

LUNCH

STRONG SNACK

DINNER

MAKE IT COUNT MOVEMENT

SPLURGE REPORT

FOLLOW-UP FRIDAY
Have a Fabulous Friday!

TODAY'S TOP 3 TASKS

....

....

....

PRAY FOR:

PAY FOR:

GRATEFUL FOR:

COMMIT TO MEMORY

THIS WEEK'S GOAL UPDATE

DATE: ....

LAST NIGHT'S HOURS OF SLEEP

○ ○ ○
○ ○ ○
○ ○ ○
○ ○ ○

REAL WATER

MEALS

BREAKFAST

LUNCH

STRONG SNACK

DINNER

MAKE IT COUNT MOVEMENT

SPLURGE REPORT

30

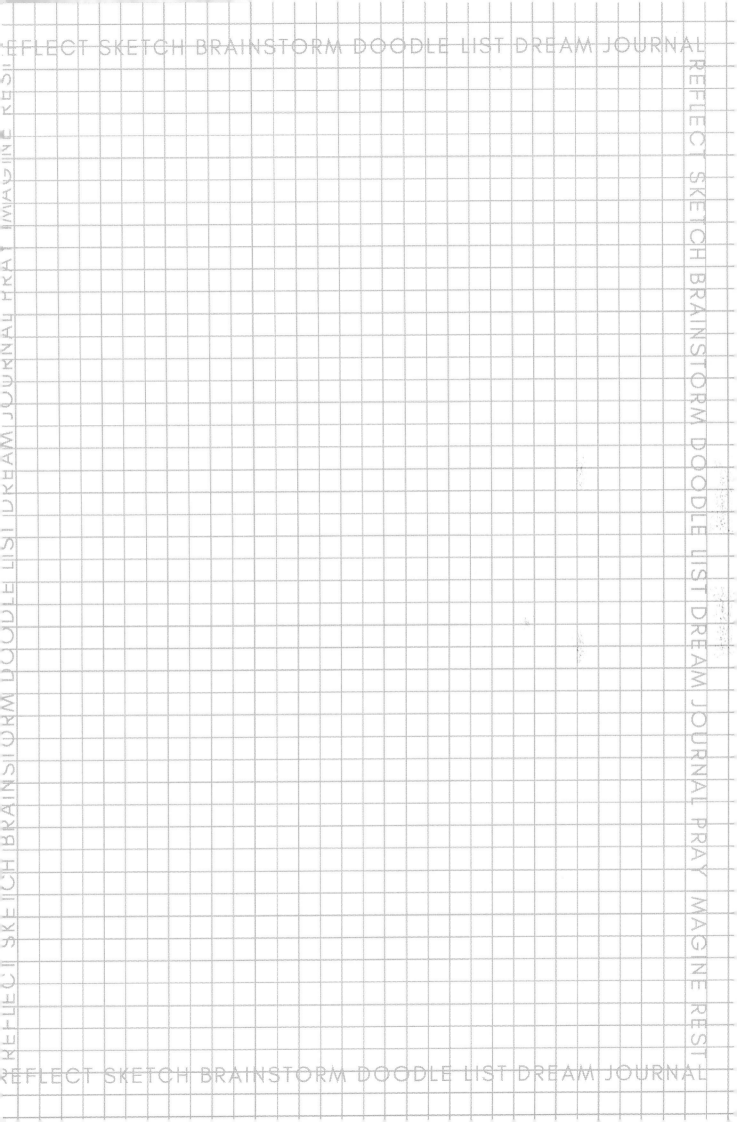

RECIPE-SWAP SATURDAY

share in **RESOLVE** *group*

TODAY'S TOP 3 TASKS

....

....

....

PRAY FOR:

PAY FOR:

GRATEFUL FOR:

COMMIT TO MEMORY

WEEKLY FOCUS REMINDER

LAST NIGHT'S HOURS OF SLEEP

REAL WATER

MEALS

BREAKFAST

LUNCH

STRONG SNACK

DINNER

MAKE IT COUNT MOVEMENT

SPLURGE REPORT

SLIP-IT-ON SUNDAY

share in **RESOLVE** *group*

TODAY'S TOP 3 TASKS

....
....
....

PRAY FOR:

PAY FOR:

GRATEFUL FOR:

COMMIT TO MEMORY

WEEKLY FOCUS REMINDER

DATE: ....

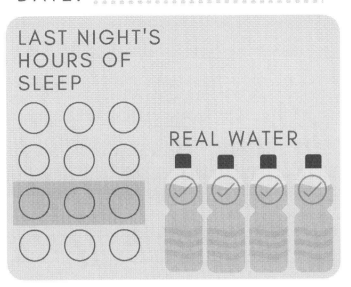

LAST NIGHT'S HOURS OF SLEEP

REAL WATER

MEALS

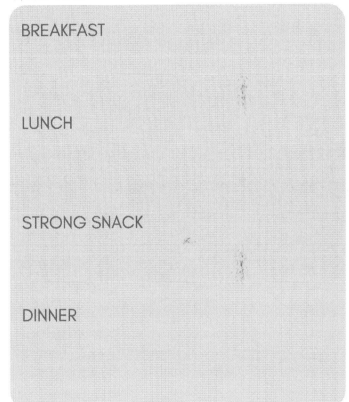

BREAKFAST

LUNCH

STRONG SNACK

DINNER

MAKE IT COUNT MOVEMENT

SPLURGE REPORT

WEEK AT A GLANCE

OVERARCHING WEEKLY FOCUS

⊚ ....

WINS FROM LAST WEEK

WHAT DIDN'T WORK?

THINGS TO GET DONE THIS WEEK:

THINGS TO GET:

THINGS TO GET RID OF:

THIS WEEK'S WORKOUTS

M ....
T ....
W ....
T ....
F ....
S ....
S ....

DATE NIGHT/QUALITY TIME

....

....

COMMIT TO MEMORY

I SEE THIS COMING:

....

....

STRATEGIC SPLURGES AHEAD

"Success is the progressive realization of a worthy goal or ideal." -Earl Nightingale

MAKE-A-PLAN MONDAY

A fresh new week with no mistakes!

TODAY'S TOP 3 TASKS

....

....

....

PRAY FOR:

PAY FOR:

GRATEFUL FOR:

SMART GOAL FOR THE WEEK

WEEKLY FOCUS REMINDER

LAST NIGHT'S HOURS OF SLEEP

REAL WATER

MEALS

BREAKFAST

LUNCH

STRONG SNACK

DINNER

MAKE IT COUNT MOVEMENT

SPLURGE REPORT

TAKE 10 TUESDAY

Be strong and courageous!

TODAY'S TOP 3 TASKS

. . . .

. . . .

PRAY FOR:

PAY FOR:

GRATEFUL FOR:

COMMIT TO MEMORY

TAKE 10 TODAY (PAGES 8-9)

DATE: . . . .

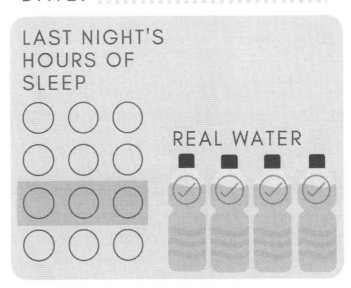

LAST NIGHT'S HOURS OF SLEEP

REAL WATER

MEALS

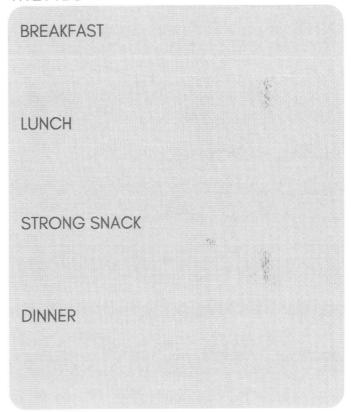

BREAKFAST

LUNCH

STRONG SNACK

DINNER

MAKE IT COUNT MOVEMENT

SPLURGE REPORT

WEDNESDAY
MID-WEEK METRIC CHECK

You're closer than you think!

TODAY'S TOP 3 TASKS

....

....

....

PRAY FOR:

PAY FOR:

GRATEFUL FOR:

COMMIT TO MEMORY

METRIC UPDATE

....

DATE: ....

LAST NIGHT'S HOURS OF SLEEP

REAL WATER

MEALS

BREAKFAST

LUNCH

STRONG SNACK

DINNER

MAKE IT COUNT MOVEMENT

SPLURGE REPORT

THOUGHTFUL THURSDAY

listen with your eyes

TODAY'S TOP 3 TASKS

....

....

....

PRAY FOR:

PAY FOR:

GRATEFUL FOR:

REACH OUT TO CHECK ON:

WEEKLY FOCUS REMINDER

listen with your eyes · · · · · · · · 39

DATE: ....

LAST NIGHT'S HOURS OF SLEEP

◯ ◯ ◯
◯ ◯ ◯
◯ ◯ ◯
◯ ◯ ◯

REAL WATER

☑ ☑ ☑ ☑

MEALS

BREAKFAST

LUNCH

STRONG SNACK

DINNER

MAKE IT COUNT MOVEMENT

SPLURGE REPORT

FOLLOW-UP FRIDAY

Believe in yourself!

TODAY'S TOP 3 TASKS

································
································
································

PRAY FOR:

PAY FOR:

GRATEFUL FOR:

COMMIT TO MEMORY

THIS WEEK'S GOAL UPDATE

DATE: ····································

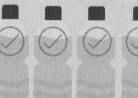

LAST NIGHT'S
HOURS OF
SLEEP

○ ○ ○
○ ○ ○
○ ○ ○
○ ○ ○

REAL WATER

✓ ✓ ✓ ✓

MEALS

BREAKFAST

LUNCH

STRONG SNACK

DINNER

MAKE IT COUNT MOVEMENT

SPLURGE REPORT

RECIPE-SWAP SATURDAY

share in  *group*

TODAY'S TOP 3 TASKS

....

....

....

PRAY FOR:

PAY FOR:

GRATEFUL FOR:

COMMIT TO MEMORY

WEEKLY FOCUS REMINDER

LAST NIGHT'S HOURS OF SLEEP

REAL WATER

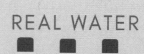

MEALS

BREAKFAST

LUNCH

STRONG SNACK

DINNER

MAKE IT COUNT MOVEMENT

SPLURGE REPORT

SLIP-IT-ON SUNDAY

share in **RESOLVE** *group*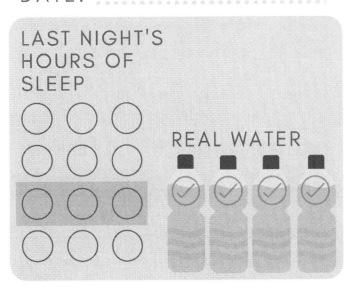

TODAY'S TOP 3 TASKS

. . . .

. . . .

DATE: . . . .

LAST NIGHT'S HOURS OF SLEEP

◯ ◯ ◯

◯ ◯ ◯

◯ ◯ ◯

◯ ◯ ◯

REAL WATER

PRAY FOR:

PAY FOR:

GRATEFUL FOR:

MEALS

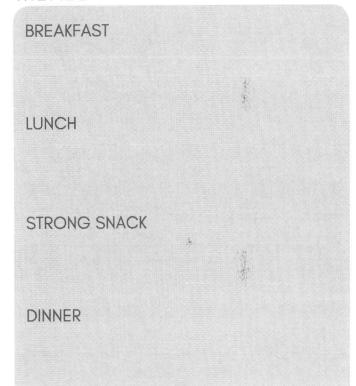

BREAKFAST

LUNCH

STRONG SNACK

DINNER

MAKE IT COUNT MOVEMENT

COMMIT TO MEMORY

WEEKLY FOCUS REMINDER

SPLURGE REPORT

WEEK AT A GLANCE

OVERARCHING WEEKLY FOCUS

....

WINS FROM LAST WEEK

WHAT DIDN'T WORK?

THINGS TO GET DONE THIS WEEK:

THINGS TO GET:

THINGS TO GET RID OF:

WEEK OF: ....

THIS WEEK'S WORKOUTS

M ....

T ....

W ....

T ....

F ....

S ....

S ....

DATE NIGHT/QUALITY TIME

....

....

COMMIT TO MEMORY

I SEE THIS COMING:

....

....

STRATEGIC SPLURGES AHEAD

Triple
S
Strategy

"Farmers who wait for perfect weather never plant. If they watch every cloud, they never harvest."
Ecclesiastes 11:4, NLT

MAKE-A-PLAN MONDAY

what you plant now will reap a harvest

TODAY'S TOP 3 TASKS

....

....

....

PRAY FOR:

PAY FOR:

GRATEFUL FOR:

SMART GOAL FOR THE WEEK

WEEKLY FOCUS REMINDER

DATE: ....

LAST NIGHT'S HOURS OF SLEEP

◯ ◯ ◯

◯ ◯ ◯

◯ ◯ ◯

◯ ◯ ◯

REAL WATER

■ ■ ■ ■
✓ ✓ ✓ ✓

MEALS

BREAKFAST

LUNCH

STRONG SNACK

DINNER

MAKE IT COUNT MOVEMENT

SPLURGE REPORT

TAKE 10 TUESDAY

I like to move-it, move-it!

TODAY'S TOP 3 TASKS

:::

:::

:::

PRAY FOR:

PAY FOR:

GRATEFUL FOR:

COMMIT TO MEMORY

TAKE 10 TODAY (PAGES 8-9)

DATE: ....

LAST NIGHT'S HOURS OF SLEEP

REAL WATER

MEALS

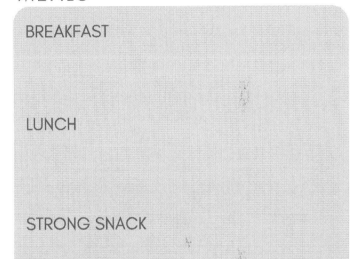

BREAKFAST

LUNCH

STRONG SNACK

DINNER

MAKE IT COUNT MOVEMENT

SPLURGE REPORT

WEDNESDAY
MID-WEEK METRIC CHECK

Look how far you have come!

TODAY'S TOP 3 TASKS

....

....

....

PRAY FOR:

PAY FOR:

GRATEFUL FOR:

COMMIT TO MEMORY

METRIC UPDATE

....

DATE: ....

LAST NIGHT'S HOURS OF SLEEP

○ ○ ○

○ ○ ○

○ ○ ○

○ ○ ○

REAL WATER

MEALS

BREAKFAST

LUNCH

STRONG SNACK

DINNER

MAKE IT COUNT MOVEMENT

SPLURGE REPORT

THOUGHTFUL THURSDAY

God changes caterpillars into butterflies

TODAY'S TOP 3 TASKS

·····································
·····································
·····································

LAST NIGHT'S HOURS OF SLEEP

REAL WATER

PRAY FOR:

PAY FOR:

GRATEFUL FOR:

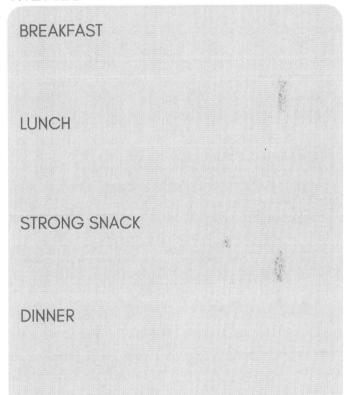

MEALS

BREAKFAST

LUNCH

STRONG SNACK

DINNER

MAKE IT COUNT MOVEMENT

REACH OUT TO CHECK ON:

SPLURGE REPORT

WEEKLY FOCUS REMINDER

·····································

FOLLOW-UP FRIDAY

You should be proud of you!

TODAY'S TOP 3 TASKS

....

....

....

PRAY FOR:

PAY FOR:

GRATEFUL FOR:

COMMIT TO MEMORY

THIS WEEK'S GOAL UPDATE

....

DATE: ....

LAST NIGHT'S HOURS OF SLEEP

REAL WATER

MEALS

BREAKFAST

LUNCH

STRONG SNACK

DINNER

MAKE IT COUNT MOVEMENT

SPLURGE REPORT

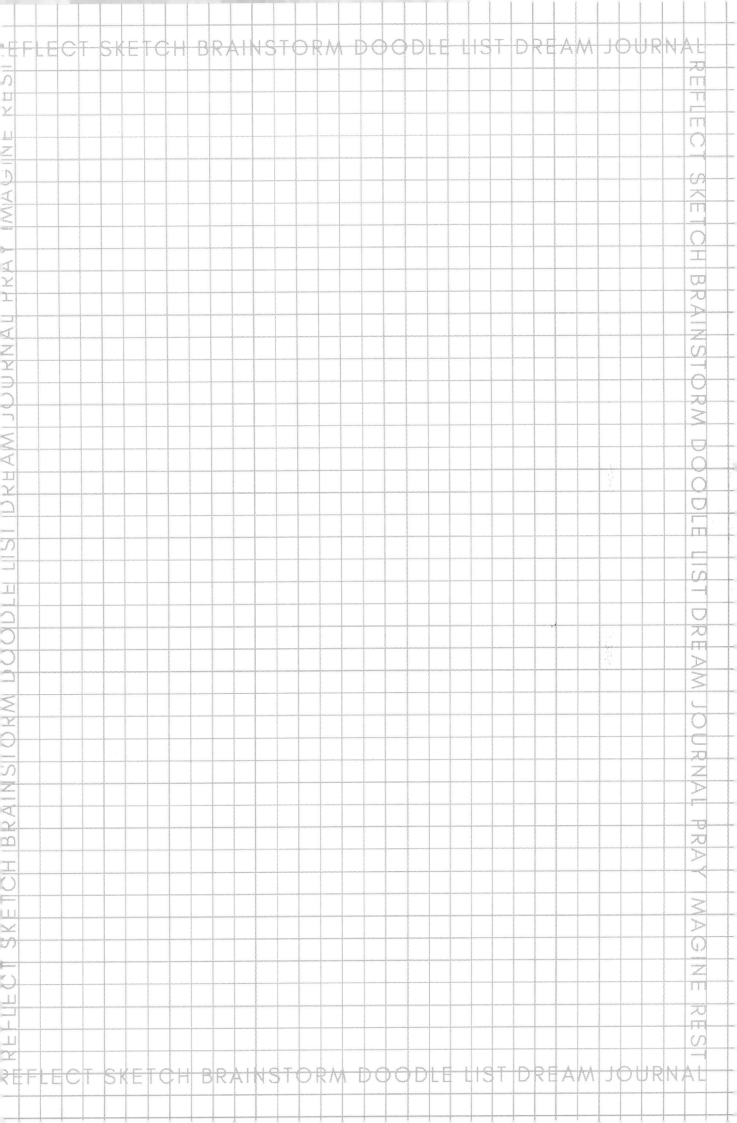

RECIPE-SWAP SATURDAY

share in **RESOLVE** *group*

TODAY'S TOP 3 TASKS

....

....

....

PRAY FOR:

PAY FOR:

GRATEFUL FOR:

COMMIT TO MEMORY

WEEKLY FOCUS REMINDER

DATE: ....

LAST NIGHT'S
HOURS OF
SLEEP

REAL WATER

MEALS

BREAKFAST

LUNCH

STRONG SNACK

DINNER

MAKE IT COUNT MOVEMENT

SPLURGE REPORT

SLIP-IT-ON SUNDAY

share in **RESOLVE** *group*

TODAY'S TOP 3 TASKS

....

....

....

PRAY FOR:

PAY FOR:

GRATEFUL FOR:

COMMIT TO MEMORY

WEEKLY FOCUS REMINDER

DATE: ....

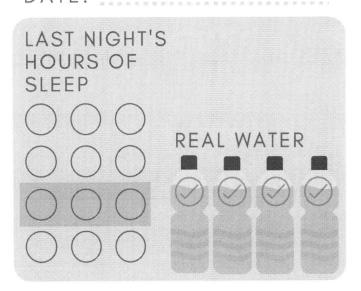

LAST NIGHT'S HOURS OF SLEEP

REAL WATER

MEALS

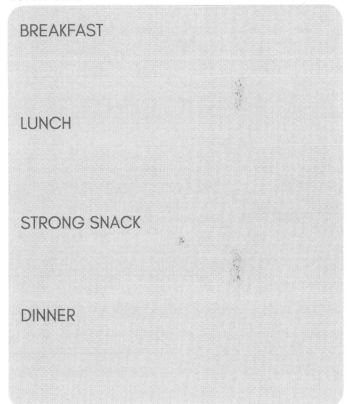

BREAKFAST

LUNCH

STRONG SNACK

DINNER

MAKE IT COUNT MOVEMENT

SPLURGE REPORT

WEEK AT A GLANCE

OVERARCHING WEEKLY FOCUS

....

WINS FROM LAST WEEK

WHAT DIDN'T WORK?

THINGS TO GET DONE THIS WEEK:

THINGS TO GET:

THINGS TO GET RID OF:

THIS WEEK'S WORKOUTS

M ....
T ....
W ....
T ....
F ....
S ....
S ....

DATE NIGHT/QUALITY TIME

....

....

COMMIT TO MEMORY

I SEE THIS COMING:

....

....

STRATEGIC SPLURGES AHEAD

Triple
S
Strategy

"Nobody who ever gave his best regretted it."
-George Halas

MAKE-A-PLAN MONDAY

Yes, you love Mondays!

TODAY'S TOP 3 TASKS

....

....

....

PRAY FOR:

PAY FOR:

GRATEFUL FOR:

SMART GOAL FOR THE WEEK

WEEKLY FOCUS REMINDER

DATE: ....

LAST NIGHT'S HOURS OF SLEEP

○ ○ ○

○ ○ ○

● ○ ○

○ ○ ○

REAL WATER

MEALS

BREAKFAST

LUNCH

STRONG SNACK

DINNER

MAKE IT COUNT MOVEMENT

SPLURGE REPORT

TAKE 10 TUESDAY

Stay strong!

TODAY'S TOP 3 TASKS

· ·

· ·

· ·

PRAY FOR:

PAY FOR:

GRATEFUL FOR:

COMMIT TO MEMORY

TAKE 10 TODAY (PAGES 8-9)

DATE: ·

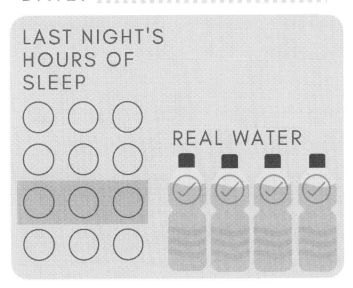

LAST NIGHT'S HOURS OF SLEEP

REAL WATER

MEALS

BREAKFAST

LUNCH

STRONG SNACK

DINNER

MAKE IT COUNT MOVEMENT

SPLURGE REPORT

WEDNESDAY
MID-WEEK METRIC CHECK
break down the goal for a breakthrough

TODAY'S TOP 3 TASKS

....
....
....

PRAY FOR:

PAY FOR:

GRATEFUL FOR:

COMMIT TO MEMORY

METRIC UPDATE

....

DATE: ....

LAST NIGHT'S HOURS OF SLEEP

◯ ◯ ◯
◯ ◯ ◯
◯ ◯ ◯
◯ ◯ ◯

REAL WATER

MEALS

BREAKFAST

LUNCH

STRONG SNACK

DINNER

MAKE IT COUNT MOVEMENT

SPLURGE REPORT

THOUGHTFUL THURSDAY

Who have you said
I love you to lately?

TODAY'S TOP 3 TASKS

....

....

....

PRAY FOR:

PAY FOR:

GRATEFUL FOR:

REACH OUT TO CHECK ON:

WEEKLY FOCUS REMINDER

.

DATE: ....

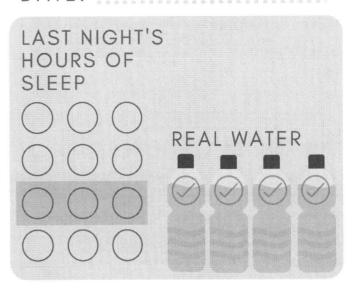

LAST NIGHT'S HOURS OF SLEEP

REAL WATER

MEALS

BREAKFAST

LUNCH

STRONG SNACK

DINNER

MAKE IT COUNT MOVEMENT

SPLURGE REPORT

FOLLOW-UP FRIDAY

You are more than enough!

TODAY'S TOP 3 TASKS

....

....

....

PRAY FOR:

PAY FOR:

GRATEFUL FOR:

COMMIT TO MEMORY

THIS WEEK'S GOAL UPDATE

....

LAST NIGHT'S HOURS OF SLEEP

REAL WATER

MEALS

BREAKFAST

LUNCH

STRONG SNACK

DINNER

MAKE IT COUNT MOVEMENT

SPLURGE REPORT

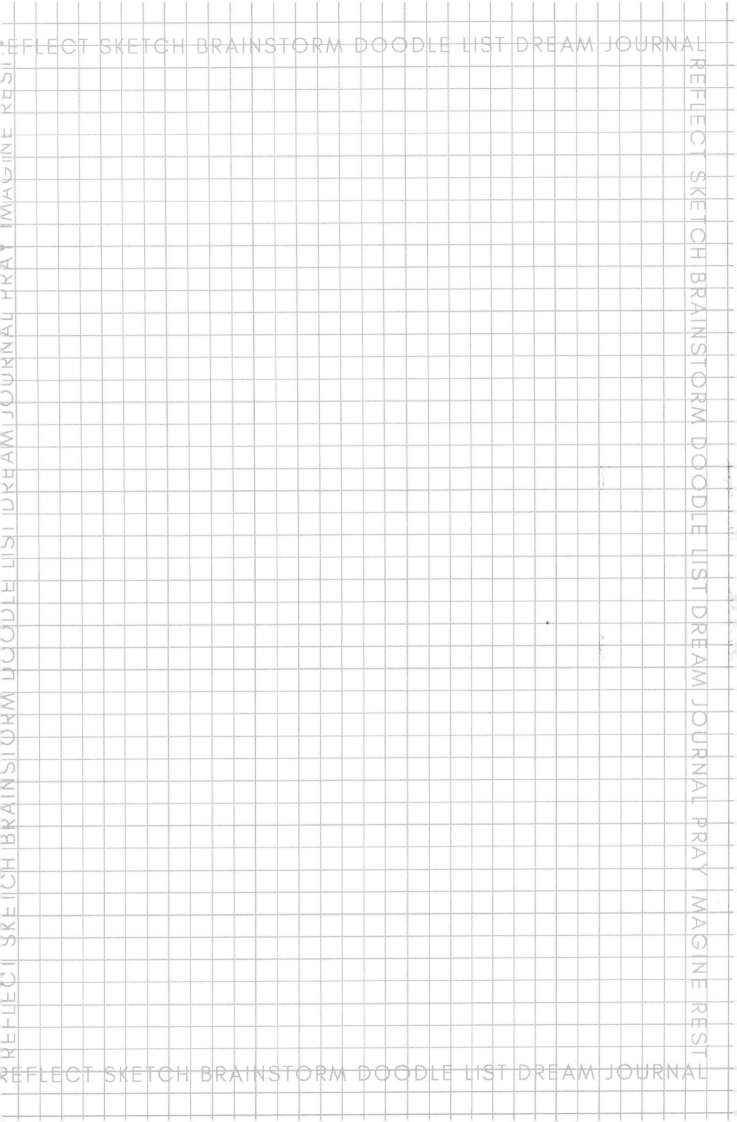

RECIPE-SWAP SATURDAY

share in R**ESOLVE** group

TODAY'S TOP 3 TASKS

....
....
....

PRAY FOR:

PAY FOR:

GRATEFUL FOR:

COMMIT TO MEMORY

WEEKLY FOCUS REMINDER

DATE: ....

LAST NIGHT'S
HOURS OF
SLEEP

○ ○ ○
○ ○ ○
○ ○ ○
○ ○ ○

REAL WATER

MEALS

BREAKFAST

LUNCH

STRONG SNACK

DINNER

MAKE IT COUNT MOVEMENT

SPLURGE REPORT

SLIP-IT-ON SUNDAY

share in **RESOLVE** *group*

TODAY'S TOP 3 TASKS

....

....

....

PRAY FOR:

PAY FOR:

GRATEFUL FOR:

COMMIT TO MEMORY

WEEKLY FOCUS REMINDER

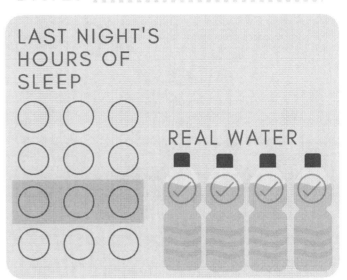

DATE: ....

LAST NIGHT'S HOURS OF SLEEP

○ ○ ○

○ ○ ○

REAL WATER

○ ○ ○

○ ○ ○

MEALS

BREAKFAST

LUNCH

STRONG SNACK

DINNER

MAKE IT COUNT MOVEMENT

SPLURGE REPORT

WEEK AT A GLANCE

OVERARCHING WEEKLY FOCUS

WINS FROM LAST WEEK

WHAT DIDN'T WORK?

THINGS TO GET DONE THIS WEEK:

THINGS TO GET:

THINGS TO GET RID OF:

THIS WEEK'S WORKOUTS

M
T
W
T
F
S
S

DATE NIGHT/QUALITY TIME

COMMIT TO MEMORY

I SEE THIS COMING:

STRATEGIC SPLURGES AHEAD

Triple
S
Strategy

"Don't judge each day by the harvest you reap but by the seeds that you plant." -Robert Louis Stevenson

MAKE-A-PLAN MONDAY

good morning, goal-getter

TODAY'S TOP 3 TASKS

....

....

....

PRAY FOR:

PAY FOR:

GRATEFUL FOR:

SMART GOAL FOR THE WEEK

WEEKLY FOCUS REMINDER

DATE: ....

LAST NIGHT'S HOURS OF SLEEP

◯ ◯ ◯
◯ ◯ ◯
◯ ◯ ◯
◯ ◯ ◯

REAL WATER

MEALS

BREAKFAST

LUNCH

STRONG SNACK

DINNER

MAKE IT COUNT MOVEMENT

SPLURGE REPORT

TAKE 10 TUESDAY

Never give up!

TODAY'S TOP 3 TASKS

....

....

PRAY FOR:

PAY FOR:

GRATEFUL FOR:

COMMIT TO MEMORY

TAKE 10 TODAY (PAGES 8-9)

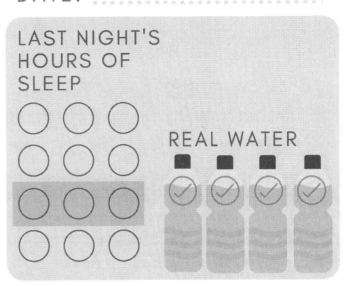

LAST NIGHT'S HOURS OF SLEEP

REAL WATER

MEALS

BREAKFAST

LUNCH

STRONG SNACK

DINNER

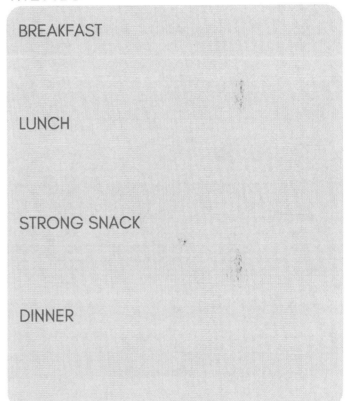

MAKE IT COUNT MOVEMENT

SPLURGE REPORT

WEDNESDAY
MID-WEEK METRIC CHECK

daily progress adds up to big results

TODAY'S TOP 3 TASKS

....

....

....

PRAY FOR:

PAY FOR:

GRATEFUL FOR:

COMMIT TO MEMORY

METRIC UPDATE

....

DATE: ....

LAST NIGHT'S HOURS OF SLEEP

○ ○ ○
○ ○ ○
○ ○ ○
○ ○ ○

REAL WATER

■ ■ ■ ■
✓ ✓ ✓ ✓

MEALS

BREAKFAST

LUNCH

STRONG SNACK

DINNER

MAKE IT COUNT MOVEMENT

SPLURGE REPORT

THOUGHTFUL THURSDAY

#accountabilityiseverything

TODAY'S TOP 3 TASKS

....

....

DATE: ....

LAST NIGHT'S HOURS OF SLEEP

◯ ◯ ◯

◯ ◯ ◯

◯ ◯ ◯

◯ ◯ ◯

REAL WATER

▪ ▪ ▪ ▪

✓ ✓ ✓ ✓

PRAY FOR:

PAY FOR:

GRATEFUL FOR:

MEALS

BREAKFAST

LUNCH

STRONG SNACK

DINNER

MAKE IT COUNT MOVEMENT

REACH OUT TO CHECK ON:

SPLURGE REPORT

WEEKLY FOCUS REMINDER

 ·································· 69

FOLLOW-UP FRIDAY

You're stronger than you know!

TODAY'S TOP 3 TASKS

....
....
....

PRAY FOR:

PAY FOR:

GRATEFUL FOR:

COMMIT TO MEMORY

THIS WEEK'S GOAL UPDATE

....

LAST NIGHT'S HOURS OF SLEEP

○ ○ ○
○ ○ ○
○ ○ ○
○ ○ ○

REAL WATER

☑ ☑ ☑ ☑

MEALS

BREAKFAST

LUNCH

STRONG SNACK

DINNER

MAKE IT COUNT MOVEMENT

SPLURGE REPORT

RECIPE-SWAP SATURDAY

 share in RESOLVE group

TODAY'S TOP 3 TASKS

....

....

....

PRAY FOR:

PAY FOR:

GRATEFUL FOR:

COMMIT TO MEMORY

WEEKLY FOCUS REMINDER

DATE: ....

LAST NIGHT'S HOURS OF SLEEP

○ ○ ○
○ ○ ○
○ ○ ○
○ ○ ○

REAL WATER

✓ ✓ ✓ ✓

MEALS

BREAKFAST

LUNCH

STRONG SNACK

DINNER

MAKE IT COUNT MOVEMENT

SPLURGE REPORT

SLIP-IT-ON SUNDAY

 *share in* **RESOLVE** *group*

TODAY'S TOP 3 TASKS

....

....

....

PRAY FOR:

PAY FOR:

GRATEFUL FOR:

COMMIT TO MEMORY

WEEKLY FOCUS REMINDER

LAST NIGHT'S HOURS OF SLEEP

REAL WATER

MEALS

BREAKFAST

LUNCH

STRONG SNACK

DINNER

MAKE IT COUNT MOVEMENT

SPLURGE REPORT

Triple **S** Strategy

WEEK AT A GLANCE

OVERARCHING WEEKLY FOCUS

....

WINS FROM LAST WEEK

WHAT DIDN'T WORK?

THINGS TO GET DONE THIS WEEK:

THINGS TO GET:

THINGS TO GET RID OF:

WEEK OF: ....

THIS WEEK'S WORKOUTS

M ....
T ....
W ....
T ....
F ....
S ....
S ....

DATE NIGHT/QUALITY TIME

....

....

COMMIT TO MEMORY

I SEE THIS COMING:

....

....

STRATEGIC SPLURGES AHEAD

Triple
S
Strategy

"Success is not final, failure is not fatal: it is the courage to continue that counts." -Winston Churchill

MAKE-A-PLAN MONDAY

You've got this!

TODAY'S TOP 3 TASKS

....

....

....

PRAY FOR:

PAY FOR:

GRATEFUL FOR:

SMART GOAL FOR THE WEEK

WEEKLY FOCUS REMINDER

DATE: ....

LAST NIGHT'S HOURS OF SLEEP

○ ○ ○

○ ○ ○

○ ○ ○

○ ○ ○

REAL WATER

✓ ✓ ✓ ✓

MEALS

BREAKFAST

LUNCH

STRONG SNACK

DINNER

MAKE IT COUNT MOVEMENT

SPLURGE REPORT

TAKE 10
TUESDAY

a cheerful heart is good medicine

TODAY'S TOP 3 TASKS

....

....

....

PRAY FOR:

PAY FOR:

GRATEFUL FOR:

COMMIT TO MEMORY

TAKE 10 TODAY (PAGES 8-9)

DATE: ....

LAST NIGHT'S HOURS OF SLEEP

REAL WATER

MEALS

BREAKFAST

LUNCH

STRONG SNACK

DINNER

MAKE IT COUNT MOVEMENT

SPLURGE REPORT

WEDNESDAY
MID-WEEK METRIC CHECK
Don't quit before you reach the best part!

TODAY'S TOP 3 TASKS

DATE:

LAST NIGHT'S HOURS OF SLEEP

○ ○ ○
○ ○ ○
○ ○ ○
○ ○ ○

REAL WATER

PRAY FOR:

PAY FOR:

GRATEFUL FOR:

MEALS

BREAKFAST

LUNCH

STRONG SNACK

DINNER

COMMIT TO MEMORY

METRIC UPDATE

MAKE IT COUNT MOVEMENT

SPLURGE REPORT

THOUGHTFUL THURSDAY

Consider how far you've come!

TODAY'S TOP 3 TASKS

....

....

....

PRAY FOR:

PAY FOR:

GRATEFUL FOR:

REACH OUT TO CHECK ON:

WEEKLY FOCUS REMINDER

DATE:

LAST NIGHT'S HOURS OF SLEEP

○ ○ ○

○ ○ ○

○ ○ ○

○ ○ ○

REAL WATER

MEALS

BREAKFAST

LUNCH

STRONG SNACK

DINNER

MAKE IT COUNT MOVEMENT

SPLURGE REPORT

FOLLOW-UP FRIDAY

Victory is in reach!

TODAY'S TOP 3 TASKS

....

....

....

PRAY FOR:

PAY FOR:

GRATEFUL FOR:

COMMIT TO MEMORY

THIS WEEK'S GOAL UPDATE

DATE: ....

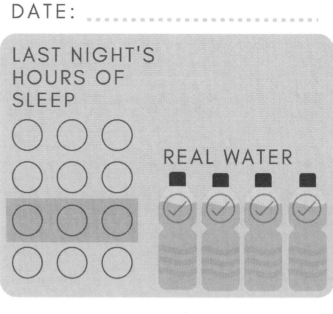

LAST NIGHT'S HOURS OF SLEEP

REAL WATER

MEALS

BREAKFAST

LUNCH

STRONG SNACK

DINNER

MAKE IT COUNT MOVEMENT

SPLURGE REPORT

RECIPE-SWAP SATURDAY

share in **RESOLVE** group

TODAY'S TOP 3 TASKS

....

....

....

PRAY FOR:

PAY FOR:

GRATEFUL FOR:

COMMIT TO MEMORY

WEEKLY FOCUS REMINDER

DATE: ....

LAST NIGHT'S
HOURS OF
SLEEP

○ ○ ○

○ ○ ○

○ ○ ○

○ ○ ○

 REAL WATER

MEALS

BREAKFAST

LUNCH

STRONG SNACK

DINNER

MAKE IT COUNT MOVEMENT

SPLURGE REPORT

SLIP-IT-ON SUNDAY

share in **RESOLVE** group

TODODAY'S TOP 3 TASKS

. . . .

. . . .

. . . .

PRAY FOR:

PAY FOR:

GRATEFUL FOR:

COMMIT TO MEMORY

WEEKLY FOCUS REMINDER

DATE: ....

LAST NIGHT'S HOURS OF SLEEP

REAL WATER

MEALS

BREAKFAST

LUNCH

STRONG SNACK

DINNER

MAKE IT COUNT MOVEMENT

SPLURGE REPORT

WEEK AT A GLANCE

OVERARCHING WEEKLY FOCUS

....

WINS FROM LAST WEEK

WHAT DIDN'T WORK?

THINGS TO GET DONE THIS WEEK:

THINGS TO GET:

THINGS TO GET RID OF:

THIS WEEK'S WORKOUTS

M ....
T ....
W ....
T ....
F ....
S ....
S ....

DATE NIGHT/QUALITY TIME

....

....

COMMIT TO MEMORY

I SEE THIS COMING:

....

....

STRATEGIC SPLURGES AHEAD

Triple **S** Strategy

"In light of my past experiences, my current circumstances, and my future hopes and dreams, what's the wise thing to do?"
-Andy Stanley

MAKE-A-PLAN MONDAY

Just master the day!

TODAY'S TOP 3 TASKS

....

....

PRAY FOR:

PAY FOR:

GRATEFUL FOR:

SMART GOAL FOR THE WEEK

WEEKLY FOCUS REMINDER

....

DATE: ....

LAST NIGHT'S HOURS OF SLEEP

○ ○ ○
○ ○ ○
○ ○ ○
○ ○ ○

REAL WATER

MEALS

BREAKFAST

LUNCH

STRONG SNACK

DINNER

MAKE IT COUNT MOVEMENT

SPLURGE REPORT

TAKE 10 TUESDAY

You were made to do big things!

TODAY'S TOP 3 TASKS

LAST NIGHT'S HOURS OF SLEEP

○ ○ ○

○ ○ ○

○ ○ ○

○ ○ ○

REAL WATER

☑ ☑ ☑ ☑

PRAY FOR:

PAY FOR:

GRATEFUL FOR:

MEALS

BREAKFAST

LUNCH

STRONG SNACK

DINNER

MAKE IT COUNT MOVEMENT

COMMIT TO MEMORY

SPLURGE REPORT

TAKE 10 TODAY (PAGES 8-9)

WEDNESDAY
MID-WEEK METRIC CHECK

#progressnotperfection

TODAY'S TOP 3 TASKS

....

....

....

PRAY FOR:

PAY FOR:

GRATEFUL FOR:

COMMIT TO MEMORY

METRIC UPDATE

....

DATE: ....

LAST NIGHT'S HOURS OF SLEEP

○ ○ ○
○ ○ ○
○ ○ ○
○ ○ ○

REAL WATER

■ ■ ■ ■
✓ ✓ ✓ ✓

MEALS

BREAKFAST

LUNCH

STRONG SNACK

DINNER

MAKE IT COUNT MOVEMENT

SPLURGE REPORT

THOUGHTFUL THURSDAY

You are of great value!

TODAY'S TOP 3 TASKS

....

....

....

PRAY FOR:

PAY FOR:

GRATEFUL FOR:

REACH OUT TO CHECK ON:

WEEKLY FOCUS REMINDER

DATE: ....

LAST NIGHT'S HOURS OF SLEEP

○ ○ ○

○ ○ ○

○ ○ ○

○ ○ ○

REAL WATER

☑ ☑ ☑ ☑

MEALS

BREAKFAST

LUNCH

STRONG SNACK

DINNER

MAKE IT COUNT MOVEMENT

SPLURGE REPORT

FOLLOW-UP FRIDAY

Work in progress!

TODAY'S TOP 3 TASKS

....

....

....

PRAY FOR:

PAY FOR:

GRATEFUL FOR:

COMMIT TO MEMORY

THIS WEEK'S GOAL UPDATE

DATE: ....

LAST NIGHT'S HOURS OF SLEEP

○ ○ ○

○ ○ ○

○ ○ ○

○ ○ ○

REAL WATER

✓ ✓ ✓ ✓

MEALS

BREAKFAST

LUNCH

STRONG SNACK

DINNER

MAKE IT COUNT MOVEMENT

SPLURGE REPORT

RECIPE-SWAP SATURDAY

 *share in* **RESOLVE** *group*

TODAY'S TOP 3 TASKS

· ·

· ·

· ·

PRAY FOR:

PAY FOR:

GRATEFUL FOR:

COMMIT TO MEMORY

WEEKLY FOCUS REMINDER

DATE: ·

LAST NIGHT'S HOURS OF SLEEP

REAL WATER

MEALS

BREAKFAST

LUNCH

STRONG SNACK

DINNER

MAKE IT COUNT MOVEMENT

SPLURGE REPORT

SLIP-IT-ON SUNDAY

share in **RESOLVE** *group*

TODAY'S TOP 3 TASKS

....

....

....

PRAY FOR:

PAY FOR:

GRATEFUL FOR:

COMMIT TO MEMORY

WEEKLY FOCUS REMINDER

DATE: ....

LAST NIGHT'S HOURS OF SLEEP

REAL WATER

MEALS

BREAKFAST

LUNCH

STRONG SNACK

DINNER

MAKE IT COUNT MOVEMENT

SPLURGE REPORT

WEEK AT A GLANCE

OVERARCHING WEEKLY FOCUS

....

WINS FROM LAST WEEK

WHAT DIDN'T WORK?

THINGS TO GET DONE THIS WEEK:

THINGS TO GET:

THINGS TO GET RID OF:

THIS WEEK'S WORKOUTS

M ....
T ....
W ....
T ....
F ....
S ....
S ....

DATE NIGHT/QUALITY TIME

....

....

COMMIT TO MEMORY

I SEE THIS COMING:

....

....

STRATEGIC SPLURGES AHEAD

Triple
S
Strategy

"It takes as much energy to wish as it does to plan."
-Eleanor Roosevelt

MAKE-A-PLAN MONDAY

Eyes on the prize!

TODAY'S TOP 3 TASKS

....

....

....

PRAY FOR:

PAY FOR:

GRATEFUL FOR:

SMART GOAL FOR THE WEEK

WEEKLY FOCUS REMINDER

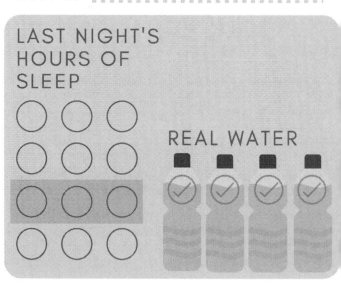

DATE: ....

LAST NIGHT'S HOURS OF SLEEP

REAL WATER

MEALS

BREAKFAST

LUNCH

STRONG SNACK

DINNER

MAKE IT COUNT MOVEMENT

SPLURGE REPORT

TAKE 10
TUESDAY

you only fail if you stop trying

TODAY'S TOP 3 TASKS

LAST NIGHT'S
HOURS OF
SLEEP

◯ ◯ ◯
◯ ◯ ◯
◯ ◯ ◯
◯ ◯ ◯

REAL WATER

■ ■ ■ ■
✓ ✓ ✓ ✓

PRAY FOR:

PAY FOR:

GRATEFUL FOR:

MEALS

BREAKFAST

LUNCH

STRONG SNACK

DINNER

COMMIT TO MEMORY

MAKE IT COUNT MOVEMENT

SPLURGE REPORT

TAKE 10 TODAY (PAGES 8-9)

WEDNESDAY
MID-WEEK METRIC CHECK

Celebrate non-scale victories!

TODAY'S TOP 3 TASKS

....

....

....

PRAY FOR:

PAY FOR:

GRATEFUL FOR:

COMMIT TO MEMORY

METRIC UPDATE

DATE: ....

LAST NIGHT'S HOURS OF SLEEP

○ ○ ○

○ ○ ○

○ ○ ○

○ ○ ○

REAL WATER

✓ ✓ ✓ ✓

MEALS

BREAKFAST

LUNCH

STRONG SNACK

DINNER

MAKE IT COUNT MOVEMENT

SPLURGE REPORT

THOUGHTFUL THURSDAY

for everything there is a season

TODAY'S TOP 3 TASKS

....

....

....

PRAY FOR:

PAY FOR:

GRATEFUL FOR:

REACH OUT TO CHECK ON:

WEEKLY FOCUS REMINDER

DATE: ....

LAST NIGHT'S HOURS OF SLEEP

○ ○ ○
○ ○ ○
○ ○ ○
○ ○ ○

REAL WATER

■ ■ ■ ■
✓ ✓ ✓ ✓

MEALS

BREAKFAST

LUNCH

STRONG SNACK

DINNER

MAKE IT COUNT MOVEMENT

SPLURGE REPORT

FOLLOW-UP FRIDAY

do not let your heart be troubled

TODAY'S TOP 3 TASKS

....
....
....

PRAY FOR:

PAY FOR:

GRATEFUL FOR:

COMMIT TO MEMORY

THIS WEEK'S GOAL UPDATE

LAST NIGHT'S HOURS OF SLEEP

○ ○ ○
○ ○ ○
○ ○ ○
○ ○ ○

REAL WATER

◼ ◼ ◼ ◼
✓ ✓ ✓ ✓

MEALS

BREAKFAST

LUNCH

STRONG SNACK

DINNER

MAKE IT COUNT MOVEMENT

SPLURGE REPORT

Triple
S
Strategy

RECIPE-SWAP SATURDAY

share in RESOLVE group

TODAY'S TOP 3 TASKS

....

....

....

PRAY FOR:

PAY FOR:

GRATEFUL FOR:

COMMIT TO MEMORY

WEEKLY FOCUS REMINDER

DATE: ....

LAST NIGHT'S HOURS OF SLEEP

◯ ◯ ◯
◯ ◯ ◯
◯ ◯ ◯
◯ ◯ ◯

REAL WATER
■ ■ ■ ■
✓ ✓ ✓ ✓

MEALS

BREAKFAST

LUNCH

STRONG SNACK

DINNER

MAKE IT COUNT MOVEMENT

SPLURGE REPORT

Triple
S
Strategy

102

SLIP-IT-ON SUNDAY

share in **RESOLVE** *group* →

TODAY'S TOP 3 TASKS

....
....
....

PRAY FOR:

PAY FOR:

GRATEFUL FOR:

COMMIT TO MEMORY

WEEKLY FOCUS REMINDER

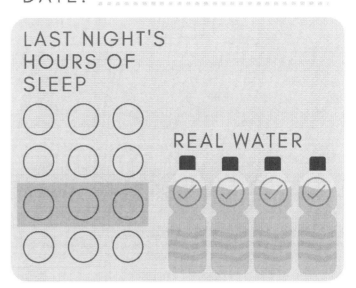

DATE: ....

LAST NIGHT'S HOURS OF SLEEP

◯ ◯ ◯
◯ ◯ ◯
◯ ◯ ◯
◯ ◯ ◯

REAL WATER

✓ ✓ ✓ ✓

MEALS

BREAKFAST

LUNCH

STRONG SNACK

DINNER

MAKE IT COUNT MOVEMENT

SPLURGE REPORT

Triple S Strategy

WEEK AT A GLANCE

OVERARCHING WEEKLY FOCUS

....

WINS FROM LAST WEEK

WHAT DIDN'T WORK?

THINGS TO GET DONE THIS WEEK:

THINGS TO GET:

THINGS TO GET RID OF:

THIS WEEK'S WORKOUTS

M ....
T ....
W ....
T ....
F ....
S ....
S ....

DATE NIGHT/QUALITY TIME

....
....

COMMIT TO MEMORY

I SEE THIS COMING:

....
....

STRATEGIC SPLURGES AHEAD

"I long to accomplish a great and noble task, but it is my chief duty to accomplish small tasks as if they were great and noble." -Helen Keller

MAKE-A-PLAN MONDAY

You are worth it!

TODAY'S TOP 3 TASKS

DATE: ....

LAST NIGHT'S HOURS OF SLEEP

○ ○ ○
○ ○ ○
○ ○ ○
○ ○ ○

REAL WATER

PRAY FOR:

PAY FOR:

GRATEFUL FOR:

MEALS

BREAKFAST

LUNCH

STRONG SNACK

DINNER

MAKE IT COUNT MOVEMENT

SMART GOAL FOR THE WEEK

SPLURGE REPORT

WEEKLY FOCUS REMINDER

TAKE 10 TUESDAY

be excellent at what is good

TODAY'S TOP 3 TASKS

PRAY FOR:

PAY FOR:

GRATEFUL FOR:

COMMIT TO MEMORY

TAKE 10 TODAY (PAGES 8-9)

LAST NIGHT'S HOURS OF SLEEP

REAL WATER

MEALS

BREAKFAST

LUNCH

STRONG SNACK

DINNER

MAKE IT COUNT MOVEMENT

SPLURGE REPORT

WEDNESDAY
MID-WEEK METRIC CHECK

if you fall, fall forward
(aka progress)

TODAY'S TOP 3 TASKS

....

....

....

PRAY FOR:

PAY FOR:

GRATEFUL FOR:

COMMIT TO MEMORY

METRIC UPDATE

....

DATE: ....

LAST NIGHT'S HOURS OF SLEEP

REAL WATER

MEALS

BREAKFAST

LUNCH

STRONG SNACK

DINNER

MAKE IT COUNT MOVEMENT

SPLURGE REPORT

THOUGHTFUL THURSDAY

#bettertogether

TODAY'S TOP 3 TASKS

....
....

DATE: ....

LAST NIGHT'S HOURS OF SLEEP

○ ○ ○
○ ○ ○
○ ○ ○
○ ○ ○

REAL WATER

☑ ☑ ☑ ☑

PRAY FOR:

PAY FOR:

GRATEFUL FOR:

MEALS

BREAKFAST

LUNCH

STRONG SNACK

DINNER

MAKE IT COUNT MOVEMENT

REACH OUT TO CHECK ON:

SPLURGE REPORT

WEEKLY FOCUS REMINDER

FOLLOW-UP FRIDAY

Be joyful in hope!

TODAY'S TOP 3 TASKS

....

....

....

PRAY FOR:

PAY FOR:

GRATEFUL FOR:

COMMIT TO MEMORY

THIS WEEK'S GOAL UPDATE

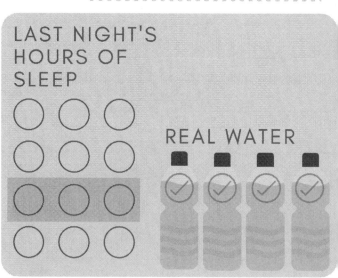

LAST NIGHT'S HOURS OF SLEEP

REAL WATER

MEALS

BREAKFAST

LUNCH

STRONG SNACK

DINNER

MAKE IT COUNT MOVEMENT

SPLURGE REPORT

RECIPE-SWAP SATURDAY

share in **RESOLVE** group

TODAY'S TOP 3 TASKS

....

....

....

PRAY FOR:

PAY FOR:

GRATEFUL FOR:

COMMIT TO MEMORY

WEEKLY FOCUS REMINDER

DATE: ....

LAST NIGHT'S
HOURS OF
SLEEP

◯ ◯ ◯

◯ ◯ ◯

◯ ◯ ◯

◯ ◯ ◯

REAL WATER

◼ ◼ ◼ ◼

✓ ✓ ✓ ✓

MEALS

BREAKFAST

LUNCH

STRONG SNACK

DINNER

MAKE IT COUNT MOVEMENT

SPLURGE REPORT

SLIP-IT-ON SUNDAY

share in **RESOLVE** *group*

TODAY'S TOP 3 TASKS

....
....
....

PRAY FOR:

PAY FOR:

GRATEFUL FOR:

COMMIT TO MEMORY

WEEKLY FOCUS REMINDER

....

DATE: ....

LAST NIGHT'S HOURS OF SLEEP

○ ○ ○
○ ○ ○
○ ○ ○
○ ○ ○

REAL WATER

☑ ☑ ☑ ☑

MEALS

BREAKFAST

LUNCH

STRONG SNACK

DINNER

MAKE IT COUNT MOVEMENT

SPLURGE REPORT

WEEK AT A GLANCE

OVERARCHING WEEKLY FOCUS

WINS FROM LAST WEEK

WHAT DIDN'T WORK?

THINGS TO GET DONE THIS WEEK:

THINGS TO GET:

THINGS TO GET RID OF:

WEEK OF: ....

THIS WEEK'S WORKOUTS

M ....
T ....
W ....
T ....
F ....
S ....
S ....

DATE NIGHT/QUALITY TIME

COMMIT TO MEMORY

I SEE THIS COMING:

STRATEGIC SPLURGES AHEAD

Triple **S** Strategy

"We cannot solve our problems with the same thinking we used when we created them." -Albert Einstein

MAKE-A-PLAN MONDAY

Shine all day!

TODAY'S TOP 3 TASKS

· ·

· ·

· ·

PRAY FOR:

PAY FOR:

GRATEFUL FOR:

SMART GOAL FOR THE WEEK

WEEKLY FOCUS REMINDER

DATE: ·

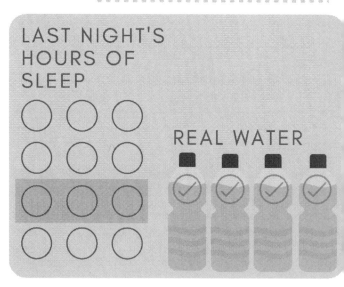

LAST NIGHT'S HOURS OF SLEEP

REAL WATER

MEALS

BREAKFAST

LUNCH

STRONG SNACK

DINNER

MAKE IT COUNT MOVEMENT

SPLURGE REPORT

TAKE 10 TUESDAY

you are beautiful inside and out

TODAY'S TOP 3 TASKS

....
....
....

PRAY FOR:

PAY FOR:

GRATEFUL FOR:

COMMIT TO MEMORY

TAKE 10 TODAY (PAGES 8-9)

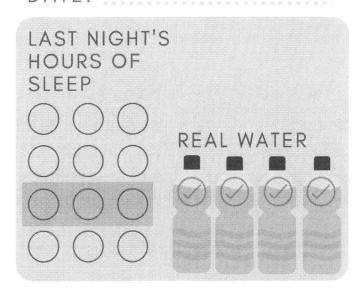

LAST NIGHT'S HOURS OF SLEEP

REAL WATER

MEALS

BREAKFAST

LUNCH

STRONG SNACK

DINNER

MAKE IT COUNT MOVEMENT

SPLURGE REPORT

Triple **S** Strategy

WEDNESDAY
MID-WEEK METRIC CHECK

experience is the best teacher

TODAY'S TOP 3 TASKS

....

....

....

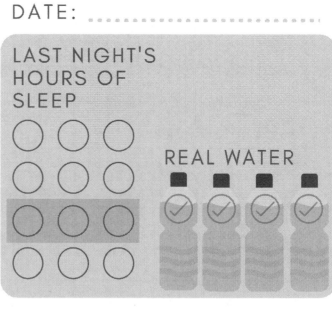

LAST NIGHT'S HOURS OF SLEEP

○ ○ ○

○ ○ ○

○ ○ ○

○ ○ ○

REAL WATER

PRAY FOR:

PAY FOR:

GRATEFUL FOR:

MEALS

BREAKFAST

LUNCH

STRONG SNACK

DINNER

COMMIT TO MEMORY

MAKE IT COUNT MOVEMENT

SPLURGE REPORT

METRIC UPDATE

experience is the best teacher

THOUGHTFUL THURSDAY

You bring the sunshine!

TODAY'S TOP 3 TASKS

....
....
....

PRAY FOR:

PAY FOR:

GRATEFUL FOR:

REACH OUT TO CHECK ON:

WEEKLY FOCUS REMINDER

DATE: ....

LAST NIGHT'S HOURS OF SLEEP

◯ ◯ ◯
◯ ◯ ◯
◯ ◯ ◯
◯ ◯ ◯

REAL WATER

☑ ☑ ☑ ☑

MEALS

BREAKFAST

LUNCH

STRONG SNACK

DINNER

MAKE IT COUNT MOVEMENT

SPLURGE REPORT

FOLLOW-UP FRIDAY

You are amazing!

TODAY'S TOP 3 TASKS

....

....

....

PRAY FOR:

PAY FOR:

GRATEFUL FOR:

COMMIT TO MEMORY

THIS WEEK'S GOAL UPDATE

....

LAST NIGHT'S HOURS OF SLEEP

○ ○ ○

○ ○ ○

○ ○ ○

○ ○ ○

REAL WATER

MEALS

BREAKFAST

LUNCH

STRONG SNACK

DINNER

MAKE IT COUNT MOVEMENT

SPLURGE REPORT

RECIPE-SWAP SATURDAY

share in R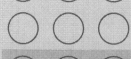ESOLVE *group*

TODAY'S TOP 3 TASKS

· ·

· ·

· ·

PRAY FOR:

PAY FOR:

GRATEFUL FOR:

COMMIT TO MEMORY

WEEKLY FOCUS REMINDER

LAST NIGHT'S HOURS OF SLEEP

REAL WATER

MEALS

BREAKFAST

LUNCH

STRONG SNACK

DINNER

MAKE IT COUNT MOVEMENT

SPLURGE REPORT

SLIP-IT-ON SUNDAY

share in **RESOLVE** group

TODAY'S TOP 3 TASKS

LAST NIGHT'S HOURS OF SLEEP

REAL WATER

PRAY FOR:

PAY FOR:

GRATEFUL FOR:

MEALS

BREAKFAST

LUNCH

STRONG SNACK

DINNER

MAKE IT COUNT MOVEMENT

COMMIT TO MEMORY

SPLURGE REPORT

WEEKLY FOCUS REMINDER

share in **RESOLVE** group

WEEK AT A GLANCE

OVERARCHING WEEKLY FOCUS

....

WINS FROM LAST WEEK

WHAT DIDN'T WORK?

THINGS TO GET DONE THIS WEEK:

THINGS TO GET:

THINGS TO GET RID OF:

WEEK OF: ....

THIS WEEK'S WORKOUTS

M
T
W
T
F
S
S

DATE NIGHT/QUALITY TIME

....

....

COMMIT TO MEMORY

I SEE THIS COMING:

....

....

STRATEGIC SPLURGES AHEAD

"Your Best YOU: Consistency + Accountability + Daily imperfect progress." -Sohailla Digsby

MAKE-A-PLAN MONDAY

Stay positive!

TODAY'S TOP 3 TASKS

....
....
....

PRAY FOR:

PAY FOR:

GRATEFUL FOR:

SMART GOAL FOR THE WEEK

WEEKLY FOCUS REMINDER

DATE: ....

LAST NIGHT'S HOURS OF SLEEP

○ ○ ○
○ ○ ○
○ ○ ○
○ ○ ○

REAL WATER

MEALS

BREAKFAST

LUNCH

STRONG SNACK

DINNER

MAKE IT COUNT MOVEMENT

SPLURGE REPORT

TAKE 10 TUESDAY

*do more things by wisdom
than by force*

TODAY'S TOP 3 TASKS

LAST NIGHT'S HOURS OF SLEEP

REAL WATER

PRAY FOR:

PAY FOR:

GRATEFUL FOR:

MEALS

BREAKFAST

LUNCH

STRONG SNACK

DINNER

MAKE IT COUNT MOVEMENT

COMMIT TO MEMORY

SPLURGE REPORT

TAKE 10 TODAY (PAGES 8-9)

WEDNESDAY
MID-WEEK METRIC CHECK
A heart at peace gives life to the body

TODAY'S TOP 3 TASKS

....

....

....

DATE: ....

LAST NIGHT'S
HOURS OF
SLEEP

○ ○ ○

○ ○ ○

○ ○ ○

○ ○ ○

REAL WATER

PRAY FOR:

PAY FOR:

GRATEFUL FOR:

COMMIT TO MEMORY

METRIC UPDATE

MEALS

BREAKFAST

LUNCH

STRONG SNACK

DINNER

MAKE IT COUNT MOVEMENT

SPLURGE REPORT

THOUGHTFUL THURSDAY

selflessness is good for your soul

TODAY'S TOP 3 TASKS

....

....

....

PRAY FOR:

PAY FOR:

GRATEFUL FOR:

REACH OUT TO CHECK ON:

WEEKLY FOCUS REMINDER

....

DATE: ....

LAST NIGHT'S HOURS OF SLEEP

○ ○ ○
○ ○ ○
○ ○ ○
○ ○ ○

REAL WATER

☑ ☑ ☑ ☑

MEALS

BREAKFAST

LUNCH

STRONG SNACK

DINNER

MAKE IT COUNT MOVEMENT

SPLURGE REPORT

FOLLOW-UP FRIDAY

God made you a masterpiece!

TODAY'S TOP 3 TASKS

....

....

....

PRAY FOR:

PAY FOR:

GRATEFUL FOR:

COMMIT TO MEMORY

THIS WEEK'S GOAL UPDATE

LAST NIGHT'S HOURS OF SLEEP

REAL WATER

MEALS

BREAKFAST

LUNCH

STRONG SNACK

DINNER

MAKE IT COUNT MOVEMENT

SPLURGE REPORT

RECIPE-SWAP SATURDAY

share in RESOLVE group

TODAY'S TOP 3 TASKS

....
....
....

PRAY FOR:

PAY FOR:

GRATEFUL FOR:

COMMIT TO MEMORY

WEEKLY FOCUS REMINDER

DATE: ....

LAST NIGHT'S HOURS OF SLEEP

○ ○ ○
○ ○ ○
○ ○ ○
○ ○ ○

REAL WATER

✓ ✓ ✓ ✓

MEALS

BREAKFAST

LUNCH

STRONG SNACK

DINNER

MAKE IT COUNT MOVEMENT

SPLURGE REPORT

SLIP-IT-ON SUNDAY

share in **RESOLVE** group

TODAY'S TOP 3 TASKS

....

....

....

PRAY FOR:

PAY FOR:

GRATEFUL FOR:

COMMIT TO MEMORY

WEEKLY FOCUS REMINDER

DATE: ....

LAST NIGHT'S
HOURS OF
SLEEP

○ ○ ○

○ ○ ○

○ ○ ○

○ ○ ○

REAL WATER

✓ ✓ ✓ ✓

MEALS

BREAKFAST

LUNCH

STRONG SNACK

DINNER

MAKE IT COUNT MOVEMENT

SPLURGE REPORT

PRIORITY PROSPECTUS

Summarize your **5Ps** again below. They may have changed over the past 12 weeks as you've learned more about yourself. (See page 6 to compare these to your initial ideas).

MY TOP PRIORITIES

PASSIONS

PROJECTS

PROGRESS

WEIGHT	WAIST	CHOL	HDL	LDL	HGB/FER.	TRI	GLU/A1C	VIT D	THYROID

Date:

PEOPLE

FINAL THOUGHTS FOR THIS SEASON

ACKNOWLEDGEMENTS

My fabulous hubby (of 20 years as of this summer!) is always so willing to help me juggle #reallife so I can meet the needs of both my energetic school-aged kiddos and you all. (Off to a front-porch date night with Tom now...*I love you, Love.*)

I'm so grateful for my Best Body Team: Bianca and Sarah on the ready at all my random work-around-family hours, and Bethany and Sara June who are willing to do whatever comes their way.

And even though I was able to keep this Planner a secret until now, my nearest and dearest family and friends always cheer me on in all my wellness shenanigans, and I am thankful.

As one who spent 7 tough years of my young-adult life not striking the sweet balance that I sincerely pray this book will help you discover, I am honored that you chose to use my Priority Planner & Wellness Log to prioritize wisely and choose wellness over fads and frenzies.

I'm right there with you, taking life one day at a time. We can be our personal best if we combine consistency with accountability, and make daily imperfect progress...together!

I'm most grateful for the grace of Jesus Christ. The pursuit of Him and His wisdom is the greatest priority by far.

#balanceisbettter
#progressnotperfection
(let the latter be reserved for Jesus himself)

ABOUT THE AUTHOR
Sohailla Digsby, RDN, LD, CPT

Sohailla is pronounced
So-hay-lah

I am a registered dietitian, not to be limited to a "calorie statistician." I am a fitness instructor, not to be confused with a "torture conductor."

I am an author and speaker and runner because those are the best outlets for my lust for life: in other words, how I make the most of my non-stop ideas, word-flow and wiggles (I'm "naturally caffeinated").

I run support groups/communities such as RESOLVE for wellness professionals and fabulous folks like you because I just plain love people, and desire for us all to operate at our personal best in each season of life. I'm not scared of getting elbow to elbow as we lift each other up on this challenging climb we call life.

I believe the accountability of relationship is everything: it's even framed on my mantle in my home (relationship with family, friends, our Creator, and our communities). Everything I do for work and charity is about bringing people together so we can be our best selves — polished and sharpened by interaction with each other to live out our purpose. Whether we can live out our purpose in each season of life depends on our health and vitality, which is certainly more important than just a number on the scale.

The scale, however is often what ushers people into my programs and fitness classes. In my professional and personal opinion, our humps and bumps (aka excess weight) are often our ticket to wellness. Humps and bumps urge us to consider where there may be overload of various kinds in our lives, and to think how to remedy the underlying issues that got us to that place of excess, rather than just to apply a band-aid (or Spanx :).

So let's prioritize wisely together to be our best selves, so we can strategically live out the purposes to which we're each called!

Made in the USA
Columbia, SC
29 August 2019